FREE TOMORROW

FREE TOMORROW

GOOSE PUNK

To order additional copies of this book, contact:
Xlibris
1-888-795-4274
www.Xlibris.com
Orders@Xlibris.com
784277

YOU WATCH THE news, & the killer whale pods in Puget Sound are dwindling cause there's not enough salmon, & you go to work in a factory, & the salmon eggs are pouring all ovber the floor, & they're sweeping them into the garbage. That's why I lost my last job. Because, I didn't like watching the health of our local environment go down the drain so tourists could buy fish at The Pike Place Market. Who really gives a shit that people can throw fish through the air, & sell it marked up so it puts on a good show for an asshole here from Chicago, or LA. I like whales, & I think they'd like me too if my species wasn't suffocating them to feed the rich. I mean when was the last time I ate salmon. Not for a long time, & I believe it was when somebody tied a fish to my front door cause they had too many. I tried to cook it, & didn't do a very good job & ended up throwing most of it away after I got a stomach ache.

The best thing about whales is that they have bigger brains than us. They don't have an edjucation like we do, though I'm sure they're schooled by their parents on how to swim & hunt fish. Plus they probably know to stay away from us since white people have hunted all whales to the brink of extinction. I recently went into a McDonalds, & ordered a number 5 hold the straw.

The ocean's been doing some weird stuff. 20 years ago one of my brother, & my favorite places to play was a beach in Blind Bay on Shaw Is. One night there were 100 million jelly fish washing up on shore. They were the clear ones, not the red ones that sting, & we gathered them up being kids, & smashed as many as we could into jellyfish mush. I'm not saying we weren't destructive, but where on Earth did all these Jellyfish come from, & why were they just washing up on shore?

Before then every now & then we'd find a red jelly fish on the beach & we had to be carefull not to touch it, or a clear one, & we'd throw it around, but that night there were so many of them, & they just beached themselves.

Our grandfather used to tell us about Red Tide, & how you never went fishing if there were Red Tide. That just hit last week. There was this legend of Red Tide, & we had one last week. So, yes it does exist, & it's not a legend.

It always amazed me that the water in Puget Sound was green & not blue. People said that was because the tree's on the islands reflected in the water, & not the sky making the water look green. Was that true, or something our parents said to make us feel better about what was going wrong in the ecosystem then. There's plenty of tree's in the Hawiian islands, & the water's very blue there. Does it have something to do with the temparature, the plankton or is it the amount of pollution from oil tankers, or poisined river water washing into the sound? Either way there aren't enough salmon for the killer whales to eat, & they're getting sick because to meet the comercial demand, we are throwing away tons of salmon eggs that could be collected, & hatched in hatcheries for the next generation for fish.

THE SUN GETS HOTTER STILL

WE'RE HAVING ONE dry summer this year. Fire season has become a year round danger in California too. Now, in Washington the sun gets hotter still, & heat waves that were a rarity in my youth are commonplace today. The lawns are brown, & the sun is beating down. The smog that was so famous in LA back then is noticable here today, & nobody is really talking about it.

The USA has some of the most coal of any nation in the world, & for the last 3 years, it's been traveling through this town by railway non stop, & my old elementary school actually had to pick up, & move because of the noise. The kids brains were being rattled next to the train tracks. It's true, I read it in the paper.

All the coal being shipped through here is being put on ships, & going to China. How stupid of us, let alone them. China has some of the worst air quality in the world. You leave your car parked for a half an hour, & you need a car wash to see through the windsheild. Are we selling it to them cause we don't want to pump all that shit into the air when we burn it so we pass the buck onto China? Seems like it, & that's the American way, pass the buck. We must be learning from China too, just build new schools. I bet the new replacement for Madison Elementary isn't even earthquake safe so it'll collapse when the big one hits too.

The president, Mr. Trump went out of his way to state that he didn't believe in climate change as soon as he was elected, & did away with many environmental regulations that prevented the USA-holes from severe environmental neglagence. That's what it's called, SEVERE ENVIRONMENTAL NEGLAGENCE. That's why I don't drive. A car is a disposable oil can that never empties, & is always leaking. At least the bus holds a few more people, & even though it's a bigger engine all day long, it's keeping some of the traffic off the street, & that's a plus. Go public transportation.

THE FACT THAT WE BURN

THE FACT THAT we burn is the reason places where the human race exists for too long become deserts. Look at the cave paintings in The Sahara. 30,000 years ago, that place was lush grasslands. Until we came along & burned up all the wood, & killed all the deer, there was water, & plant life. Now, beautiful North America which was the home the unbelievable old growth forests is becoming a desert too. You can't say it's not because of us. We harvested this continent, & we cut down all the lumber that was keeping the ground cool. Now it's a tinderbox.

30 years ago in Canada when I was little, we had 40 degree below zero winters. It would be 40 degrees below for a month every year. These days I hear it maybe that cold for a night or two, & the pictures of the glaciers in Alaska are shocking too. They have shrank drastically, & you can't say it's not because of us. If not for our polutive influence, it's been our desire for a warmer climate taking effect. We've been wishing for a Northwest Passage for 500 years. We're getting one now.

The natives believed fire was a gift from the gods. Very well it might have been, & you know very well the gods could take it back if we don't take care of it. This country could burn corner to corner, & we could loose knowlege of fire, & I'll tell you how.

How many people don't go camping, don't barbeque with a wood fire, or don't have wood burning stoves in their houses? Lot's, so if these people are the only ones to survive a huge population decrease, & they can't start a fire. Then the human race is no better than a raccoon civilization.

As a kid in Canada, we were scared of bear attacks, & bears were feared. These days, they come into the city, & start going through the trash, & it's no big deal to anyone, & when they're found, they're just run off. The bears don't want to kill us anymore, & we're not afraid of them. Why is it that they used to rip our scalps off & now they don't? Are they learning every time they come into the city, & we run them off?

The fact is we burn, & it's definatly a different kind of heat when your sitting on a cement parking lot than under a tree, & that's why you can't deny that the human race is responsible for it being so much hotter these days. Unless you question whether the old growth forests really did exist in the first place. One question is, where did all the cut wood go? You'd think there would have been a lot of lumber after logging such a huge continent full of such vast old growth forests right?

RAIN RAIN GO AWAY

DRAUGHT WAS THE cause of The Great Depression, I believe. We cut all the sod out of the plains for farming, & no rain came. Therefore The Dirty 30's came about, & people had to eat their dogs to avoid starving. Upon the end of the Depression, Roosevelt got everyone back to work building schools & bridges in the west, & invented Social Security to prevent another depression.

When we reach a draught in the upper half now, & fall back into what can cause another depression, what kind of stress will that have on the economy when so many people are out of work we all get Social Security? If eveyone is getting the same stipend & only spending the same amount of money every month isn't that becoming socialist a little bit?

I'm not dissing Social Security, I've been on it for years because, of mental illness, but there is also a lot of people I know who are on it too who just don't work, & don't take the medication for their diagnosis either, & seem to do just fine off their meds. I have to take my meds, I feel terrible without them & I can't function. I can't sleep without it, & I'm not ok, but there's people I know who do take the meds, & people who don't & the people who don't are nothing but trouble. And mostly believe in God. God has their back, & the doctor doesn't know shit to them when he perscribes their meds, but they're fine with recieving the money. If they don't need the medication for their mental diagnosis, why can't they go work, & leave us to work with our disabilities? Things are bad enough, ration the water.

On the other hand, is contributing to society a good thing after all? Maybe these people are doing more good not contributing to a full time job, & driving a big SUV to take their artifact children to school evey morning, & never caring about money or their carbon footprint yet. It's true, they do less harm on the street doing illigal drugs than calling the shots for the WTO. I actually prefer them doing what they're doing, & not working for the man, & polluting our atmosphere or ocean with their evident carelessness.

NEVER TOO LATE

THE PLANET EARTH will exist after the extinction of the human race, & life will exist, it'll only have to adapt to new conditions on the planet. That's the beauty of life, it can adapt, & learn. Learning is an adaptation. You can learn to live in colder temparaturs when you're from the south. That's a minor adaptation. Evolution exists & I know it's true simply because we have all the different breeds of dogs. (over 200) Derived from one species of wild dog that cave men domesticated. All the different breeds of dogs look very different from each other, & have different traits. In time I believe they will breed in separate species's from each other, not just breeds. Like the finches in the Galapagos Islands. They bred to look differently to blend in. With dogs, they were bred by humans for different traits which make them better for different purposes. An early begining to an evoloution.

Wolves in England, & Europe are different than wolves in Norht American, yet I would think they could breed with each other like a dog can breed with a wolf. A dog is a different species than a wolf, yet they can breed. Just like a poodle is the same species as a St. Bernard, yet they don't breed. There isn't much difference than the finches in Galapagos Island.

The species on Earth changed with the extinctions of the dinosaurs, & grew hair to adapt to a colder climate when the dinosaurs died. Something new will evolve with our extinction, & life will prevail on Earth when we're gone no matter how bad it seems now to us when we die.

It's concieted to believe that UFO's are studying the human race, & have been for hundreds of years when new life can evolve to take our place very easily, & an event of such has taken place in the planets history before. Humans are not special, & animals learn. Even the big cats of Africa, & the elephants know their time is getting near. Just watch the video of that last male White Rhino as he's put to sleep. He knows his death is the end of an era, but life itself will prevail.

We humans are actually very good at speeding up evolution. Look at tree grafting for example. You can create an apple tree with two kinds of apples. Thus practically creating a new species by grafting bark. And now, with genetic engineering used in our food production, mutations are soon to be allowed. We've scoffed at the idea for years in TMNT videos, & Homer's job on The Simpsons, but such a thing I believe can happen due to marijuana use for example.

When I was in my teens, I get stoned with my dog, & I looked into his eyes. I followed his eyes, & he followed mine. I soon learned how to move my ears individually from each other, & now I can raise an ear to the slightest sound. Like a dog because, I learned how from a dog. I had to stretch the muscles in my scalp by stretching my neck so it would feel better, & soon I could move my ears. I can only wonder if I have children someday that they will be able to do the same, or not. My ears don't seem to hear any better, they just move. Although, coming from a farming family hearing loss runs in the family, & I have suffered none as a musician.

Whether what I've learned to do with my ears is the begining of some evolution, a mutation, or a schitzhophrenic dillusion I don't know, but I certainly couldn't do such a thing until I met eyes with a dog, who opened my eyes to such a thing while I was stoned on marijuana of all things. These days I can't smoke it anymore, I get too stoned & go catatonic, but the changes I went through have not gone away.

EVOLUTION IN VEHICLES

EVERYTHING EVOLVES, IN society too. Watch the automobile evolve as well. It's gone from a giant hunk of steel to a compact piece of plastic in under 100 years. From the remote part of Canada where my dad grew up, they still used horse & buggy when he was a kid. Now, every farmer there has a yard full of high tech machinery, & smooth running hybrid truck meeting emitions standards. A little different from the farm trucks we had as a kid which ran seasonally like the farm equipment, & we used once a year to haul hay on some occaisions now, can go accross the country 50 times on 5 tanks of gas each way.

I saw my first hybrid bus last weekend, & my new girlfriend laughed at me & said they have had those for years. News to me, & I'm really glad to hear it. Like I said earlier, the bus runs no matter what. It's good though cause it keeps the traffic down.

As technology advances, so does everything that involves a technological advance to meet our growing population, & our changing needs. Who's to say birth defects (Which are considered a disability) might somehow turn out to be an advantage to some of the children born with them.

A friend of mine when we were first diagnosed with mental illness said, "We have 'this ability', not disability". I see this as true because, he was in two bands with me & we used our mental illnesses as our creative edge, & made some really awesome music together.

We used to brain storm ideas all day long & just throw out crazy puns untill a few years into it we did the DIAGNOSED "Medicine is Business" album. I'd like to say music evolves too, techlological advances & taste change with each new generation. Starting with animal hide drums, to electronic drum machines. Music moves with the dancer.

THE MOUNTAINS

I'VE BECOME AWARE that tree's don't grow back really fast. The logging on the mountain to the East of our town shows this very evidently. There's been logging on the mountain, & it was done years ago. It still hasn't gotten any new growth back in over 20 years. There's still the same patchy, cut out missing chunks from the forests on the mountain, & it's ugly as hell. This big hill that once stood so beautiful surrounding the valley looks like it's had a bad haircut. There's definatly more than 3 days between a good haircut & a bad in this case. Same with the mountain to the South. It's called Little Mountain, & 20 years ago, it was beautiful. Then they logged part of it. With little Mountain though, I really did see some growth come back, & the chunks that were cut out of it have replaced themselves with deciduous trees, not evergreens.

You can't use hillsides like these two mountains for farmland. So, they sit there chopped to hell until something grows back, & I don't see how the price of lumber makes up for how bad the hill have looked for so long. In fact as small as these hills are, there wasn't much wood that they got off both mountains. So, why destroy our scenery for a few bucks into a pulp mill?

Clearly the answer is within the government. The government signed a document the minute Trump was elected to cut National Parks in New Mexico nearly in half. Legalizing oil drilling there. At least one of the mountains I'm talking about here is a park, & the government has to be the ones allowing the logging there too.

It's like the government basically takes the land for themselves if they want it. They took it from the Indians, & they make it a park not for the people but so they can use it for themselves down the road. That's what I saw when they cut the size of the parks in New Mexico in half.

After they log, they like to run power lines through the land once the trees are gone too. You may think there's forests for days behind your city limits, & you take a walk out there, & your hopes are crushed cause it's all been logged. There's tall grass & small deciduous trees with power lines running through it. Definatly not the once revered old growth forests that kept our continent so cool & made it the wonderfull place for the Native American's peace to thrive.

Here's some trivia; It took the white man 5,000 years to go from stone age to industrial age, & the Native Americans did it in less than 100. The idustrial age is when our pollution became a problem, & smokestacks became commonplace in places like Chicago.

Here's some more trivia; A new oil refinery hasn't been built in the USA since the late 60's. So, the price of gas isn't because there's no oil, it's because there's just as much gas being produced as there ever was, only way more cars, & people.

Most of the products you buy these days are, "Designed for the dump". It's a disposable society, & they make products so they'll break. That way you have to go buy another one. The old saying, "They don't make em like they used to" isn't so funny because, they really don't. They design them to last only a short while.

I know this is true because, I once bought a clock radio from rite aide, & assuming it would work I threw out the recipt. When I got it home it did not work so I had to throw it away & buy another one somewhere else. You can't expect anything with a guarantee written on the box to work. Thank you Chris Farley.

CONSTRUCTION FOLLOWS ME EVERYWHERE

ROAD WORK IS the most annoying thing on the planet. Along with remodeling & construction. All three of which seem to follow me everywhere. Everywhere I've lived in this country since 1993, there has been some sort of construction or roadwork a few monthes after I move in, & it usually drives me out of the place where I'm living. This means that it follows me to the new place I move. It's even been a problem when I was homeless. They were actually working on the streets where I was living. Of course that wasn't all bad, there were portable bathrooms there.

Ever seen the movie, FALLING DOWN with Michael Douglas? In that movie Michael Douglas says to a construction worker, "There's nothing wrong with this street is there?" "You just have to tear it up so you get the same budget for next year?" If this is true, I wouldn't be surprised.

You know the saying, "It's a small world"? It really is, & I've done some work doing paving right? That asphalt is very hot when it's in the machine & you are about to pave. That could be warming the atmosphere like a heater does all by itself. Blacktop is also black, & it absorbs the heat. The more of it on the road we have, the more of the suns rays are absorbed into the crust radiating heat into the air.

I once paved a driveway for a guy & it ruined the front yard he had growing. He had the most beautiful tree's & a great gravel driveway, & he called us in to pave it which ruined the whole look & polluted his garden. I couldn't believe the mistake this guy made. I still got paid though, & that's part of the problem for everybody.

Blacktop doesn't really shade the forest floor, & keep in moisture & fresh water like the canopy of an old growth forest would now does it. Since these old growth forests are depleted now, all the rain evaporates off the dirt, or is funneled into storm drains, & is circulated into the rivers & runs into the ocean. Thus collecting whatever pollutants allong the way, & polluting the ocean in the end. The old growth forests would have filtered the water, while it is now pollouted instead. And this is thanks to the industrial revolution.

BURNING PLANET EARTH

CAN YOU IMAGINE that the greenest planet with all it's plentifull water supply is in danger of burning? That's what I see in the future. The sun getting hotter & drying up the land. While the water flows into the oceans & the icecaps mealt. All the water turning to salt water, & everything living dries up & burns. Just as you thought it was starting to subside, flying saucers move in, & enslave, & study the rest of the humans & animals until they take over & inhabit the planet themselves.

When I started smoking pot, I started thinking at night when I was really stoned, & my first thought during that time was, "This country's gonna burn". I was thinking like the people would rise up & take out the elected officials at the time, but maybe this country is gonna burn, & it's gonna be forest fires. The largest fire in California history is burning right now as I'm typing.

It's true that large amounts of trees attract rainfall. So, after cutting them all down, the risk of draught is higher. So is the risk of fire. Can you imagine our once green lush planet turning into a fire ball & all life on Earth burnt to a crisp?

This is what the smoke turned the sun into last year from the forest fires. The smoke actually turned the sun red. I saw a Native American that I know walking on the reservation with a crazy look in his eye like the Gods were angry with what the white man had done to the country.

Before we cut down all the trees, a forest fire was really not that big a danger since it wouldn't burn everything in the forest. It would only burn what was on the forest floor cause the trees were so big they wouldn't burn in a fire. Now, the trees are so much smaller that the whole forest goes up when a fire is started. Not only that but they quit calling them forest fires & now they call them wildfires because probably there aren't so many forests only the grass & shrubs after we've logged all trees are burning. The fires just speed accross the land burning up all the grass & shrubs & because all the trees are gone, poof what's left is up in smoke.

Forest fires actually used to help the health of the forest because they would release nutrients in the smaller plants in the forest for the bigger trees to soak in through their roots.

I'm 1,000 miles north of the fires in California, & the moon looks sort of orange. Probably from the smoke in the atmosphere.

THE LORD OF THE FLIES

25 YEARS AGO in Washington, we didn't have any roaches in the ghetto. There wasn't any bugs in our apartment where we lived when I was a kid. Now, I'm living in a similar situation, & there's roaches like mad in here. I believe they hitched a ride on some Mexicans moving up from the south to Mount Vernon where I live & now we have these pests.

30 years ago up in Canada, none of the dogs had fleas either, & 10 years ago, last time I spent time with my father up there, there were fleas all over the dogs, & my dad was putting flea powder on them to no avail.

I believe the temperatures have warmed so much that these insects are moving north, & infesting places that they formerly couldn't survive there.

It really used to be too cold in Canada where I'm from for fleas, & now the dogs are infested with them. Along with the warmer winters comes insects which aren't killed off during the winter by the cold temperatures. Just like THE LITTLE SHOP OF HORRORS, I'm now feeding roaches to my carnivorous plant. Like I'm bring home the bodies to keep it happy.

Hopfully the Venus Fly Trap will scare the rest of these roaches back outside as it digests this one alive.

MAN I'M DARK

I GET VERY tan very easily. Skin cancer is a very real risk now that the sun is getting more direct onto our skin. I don't really believe in sun screen. I don't think it really works. I did know a guy who got skin cancer & it was caught early. A nurse pratitioner removed the cancer with him awake, & gave him a band aide & a 98% chance of survival.

I was in the hospital once, & I was in a coma. There were a bunch of East Indian women nurses who kept on coming & drawing blood out of the veins in my hands. Now, in the summer when I'm tan, I have some freckles that appear on the tops of my hands when my skin gets more tan. I really believe that the East Indian nurses gave me some of their pigment to protect me from the sun.

I know of an old story about an Ethiopian who gave the Leopard his spots. The Leopard took his skin off one night to go for a swim, & the Ethiopian came & took 3 fingers & made spots on the Leopard's skin while the Leopard was swimming. When the Leopard came back, & put his skin back on, he had spots, & that's how the Leopard got his spots.

I think this is true that the Etheopian can share his or her pigment, & that's why I have spots on the backs of my hands now. Maybe I'm the Leopard symbolicaly, or metaphorically.

When I woke up from the coma, they moved me over to the other side of the hospital, & there were more East Indian ladies working over there. I had been given a large brace for my leg, & one nurse took it to get it adjusted to fit me better. When one of the East Indian nurses asked me where it was I said a nurse had taken it, & she spoke positivly, & said, "She will bring it back". She wished a good wish, & the other nurse did bring it back. To me that's positive thinking. To speak something good into existance, rather than say, "Oh no, I'm gonna fail at that". Then by saying this you really do fail at that.

THE ANIMALS ARE TRYING NOT TO LAUGH

EVER GO TO the fair, & see the fat pigs with their asses facing the fair goers? You look a little closer and those pigs are hiding smiles when they cover their faces. Yes, the animals are trying not to laugh at all those fools. The animals know they're off to slaughter, & they know that someday the farmers fate will be at the hands of their decendents. They know what is going to happen to them is nothing compared to what will happen to the human race because of the way they've treated the animals throughout history. There's nothing a pig can do about his fate, the slaugherhouse, & we people have the chance now to change that, & only we have the chance now to change that.

Animals know, & so do I. I was born on a farm & I can see the animals like they're an equal to me. I can converse on their level & read their bodylanguage. I know just as good as them, & I can see these farmers for the fools they really are. My dad didn't care, but I do. I like the animals, & I like to see their faces. I like them, & they like me. We get each others sense of humor, & if you don't like it, fuck you! I missed those horses the minute I left the fair, & by the time I got home I'd forgotten to worry about them, & I knew it was fine.

THAT ONE CARELESS CIGARETTE BUTT

YOU KNOW, THE more dry it get in the evergreen forests, the more those needles on the trees become flamable. We used to poach dead standings off of county land for firewood, & we were always aware of that one careless cigarette butt that could burn down the state. A year later when I was in jail, (for something else) an idea for my defense was to say I used to be a volunteer fire fighter. Poaching those dead standings off county land was in a way, fire fighting. It was because we were taking dry wood out of the forests that could just burn up.

Now, the vast evergreen forests in Washington State could all go up the longer this draught goes on. It's been more dry every year for 20 or 25 years. In winter here, it used to rain all year, & I remember sitting at home waiting for a dry day just to go skateboard in the winter. These days it rains, & then it dries up right away. All the soaked in moisture is gone, & even though evergreens are always green, they're needles get dry, & more flamable this way. Just asking for that one careless cigarette butt to come along & toast the state.

You can tell how dry it is by just pulling a few needles off a tree as you walk by & feel how dry the needles are in your fingers. I found one tree today that wasn't so bad, & I was surprised. A week later, the needles are dry & brittle too. The grass around it was dry, & the dirt was dry too, it's almost too hot for a camel.

AS LIFE NON EXISTS IN COME FLYING DISCS

THERE REALLY IS no point in flattering ourselves into thinking that the human race is so important that a race of little grey men have been studying us since we evolved. The human race has exploded in the last 100 years, & before then we were relatively sparsly populated, & there weren't any reports until Roswell, & Area 51. To say that the greys created the human race 40,000 years ago like they did in that new Indiana Jones movie is too much. I really don't think they care.

It is good that the scientists are finding other planets in the universe these days, & they discovered a liquid lake on Mars. The lake is so salty it won't freeze, & it's located below the Martian Antarctic. I have a strong hope that they will find life on another planet in my lifetime. Whether it's intelligent or not & how you define intelligence is imperative but that sure will be cool to find out we're not alone.

I see through the myth that the greys are coming to abduct us all though. That's hype brought on by the media. It's also basically Hollywood, & anyone with half a brain knows not to believe everything you see on TV.

The lake on Mars is only 12 miles wide, & somehow they discovered it below the surface. I find the thought of amoboa life forms all too possible on other planets, & I'm really pushing for our scientists to make the discovery of life on other planets. I just don't think it's the greys.

A Native American once told me that there are lots of aliens that the Natives know about. Some look like greys, & some aliens look just like regular human beings. Who's to say, maybe?

SK8 OR DIE

IN WASHINGTON, WE'RE famous for raining 9 monthes out of the year. It hasn't rained that much in the last few years. In the past, when it wasn't raining at times in the winter, it was frosty, with clear skys. I liked that weather the best because it meant I could go skateboarding. Last winter, although it was cold, it wasn't really frosty at all. The cold wasn't so bad when it wasn't raining.

Now, when it's cold in winter, it gets dry then too. So, if it doesn't rain for a week, & it is cold & clear then the ground drys out. Also, it hasn't been windy. I remember waiting for the school bus in '90 & the wind would blow us down the street. That doesn't happen anymore.

I was homeless last winter, & if it were as cold as it were when I was a kid at times, I would have been miserable, & I wasn't. This is a definate climate change. Global warming or whatever, it's definatly different. I can't help but wonder what it was like before my short life began in 1981.

ONLY IN CANADA

THE AMERICAN GOVERRNMENT lies to the people. In Canada, there is widespread belief that UFO's do exist. Here in the states, it's kept hush hush. My Christian fanatic family took pictures of themselves with clouds that looked like flying saucers in the sky behind them. Canada isn't such a lying nation, & we don't lie to the people, & you better believe it, they're out there. Studying us or not, we're not alone, & the US government is saying it. They are however adding a new branch to the military. Yes, soon we will have the, "Space Force" added to the ARMY, NAVY, AIR FORCE, MARINES, & COAST GUARD. I won't be joining up.

DO THE CITY LIGHTS REALLY DROWN OUT THE STARS?

THE ANSWER IS yes. Before all the lights went up in my home town of Hythe Alberta in Northern Canada, I once saw so many stars in the sky they frightend the horses & the horses got out. We were going to have dinner at somebody elses farm, & we had to cancel because the horses were frightened out by a cluster-fuck in the sky. I saw it with my own two eyes, wall to wall stars. These days, you can't even find the big dipper in Mount Vernon.

The image of the planet from space has changed too. Yes, it's not so green anymore. It's actually quite brown when they show the image of planet Earth from space. It used to be green, I don't know what happened.

It's also coldest right before the sun comes up. I was homeless for a few years, & let me tell you, the wee hours of the morning are when you really have to huddle. It pays to get your core warm by midnight, & really huddle through the morning because those few minutes before it gets light, it's really a little colder. Is this because of our thinning atmosphere, or is it normal?

Now, I'm in an apartment, & it's summer. I get up really early every morning like between 2 & 4. When I first get up at 2, it's not so uncomfortable out on the porch when I go out to smoke, but come 5 in the morning, sometimes I have to put on a sweatshirt. I have to take it off right away when the sun comes up, & then it gets rediculously hot, but that is a fact. It's colder just before the sun comes up.

They say you feel the temperature differently in different parts of the world. This is true, & I know it cause, the cold is way different up in Hythe. 15 or 20 below doesn't feel like shit even though it's cold enough to maybe freeze to death. In Western Washington, there's always this chill in the air. Except when it's rediculously hot in the afternoon during summer. Whenever it's cool there's this annoying chill you don't feel when it's cold like a blizzard. The blizzard can kill you, & yet it's not so bad, go figure. The damp chill is Washington is enough to rot your toenails. It's like your either in the shade, & chilled or in the sun & sweating. Is the atmosphere filling with carbon dioxide? The air is much cleaner in sparsly populated Hythe Alberta according to my dad.

THERE'S AN EASY WAY & A HARD WAY TO DO EVERYTHING

THE EASY WAY to stop all this climate change, & global warming would have been to make freon gas illigal in the 80's. Then maybe our ozone would have stopped being eaten & might have repaired itself within 50 years. Unfortunatly, people do things the hard way, & we have started a warming trend that seems like it's gonna slowly cook us like frogs. You know how if you drop a frog in boiling water, it'll jump right out, but if you put it in cold water, & turn on the heat, it'll boil to death without knowing. That's what's gonna happen to us I bet. The world will just get hotter & hotter. That's why nuking somebody again might be a good idea, so we all jump right out of the water, & stop polluting.

The easy way might have been to make freon gas illigal, & it might be easier to drop the bomb on somebody. That way it'll get a little worse really fast and people might actually think, & stop this cycle of pollution worldwide. All I know is were being boiled like frogs, very slowly, & we don't really notice it yet, & won't until it's curtains. The scientists know it's not too late, so do I. For the existance of the race, drop the bomb.

NO STONE UNTURNED

THE HUMAN RACE has completely transformed the face of the planet to their liking. Ever really stop to think about any spot of land which hasn't been turned by a plow or a bucket that's exactly the way it was before humans came there? Seriously, humans have moved every spot of land on the planet. That's the reason for the Great Depression. They plowed under all the sod on the plains, & it quit raining. Seriously, just by moving the land for farming, it caused a drought & almost ended the country.

Except for the snow in Antarctica, all the land has been moved somehow for development, or logging, & the human race has done it. There's not a spot of land, (if you think about it) that hasn't been overturned. It all has been piled up or dug out, had cement built on it, or plowed for farming. Every spot of land is a little higher or a little lower than it really is meant to be.

This is mainly because we logged all the trees, & people have been changing the landscape all of their existance. Their existance which is a lot longer than the last 5,000 years I might add. You really think God created the dinosaurs, & the oil on the same day 5,000 years ago? I don't think so. Our nice green Earth might turn orange though & just burst into flames. The Space Force will be the only people who survive.

It takes 500 years for an inch of top soil to naturally accumulate on the ground, & people can speed this up with manure, & enzymes that decompose the manure faster. We build new parts of cities over the old parts though. Seattle has a underground tourist attraction where you can go & see the origional settlement that has since been built over. It seems like the Earth is growing ever so slowly. After all, I believe the Earth is a living entity itself, & we are just a parasite.

An anthill is completely built by the ants, & they make their own home. So do the bees when they build a hive. Who's to say all the development, & building on Earth by the human race isn't just as natural as an anthill, or a beehive? We've just taken off, & are over populating the planet in the last 100 years. Rabbits have a disease called 7 year fever. As you know rabbits multiply. They will multiply at a place for 7 years. Then once too many of them are living somewhere, they all die out. For 100 years the human population on Earth has been multiplying, & I fear a mass population decrease is coming. Maybe not an extinction, but something might kill off a lot of people.

When that happens, we'll have to change the way we live quite a bit, & learn how to survive all over again. It'll be evolution really cause only the strong survive. Strengthing the human race by renewing & making us have to start all over again. Extinction is possible, population decrease might be enevitable.

People might think we have to go to space on the space force because we haven't got anywhere else to go. As the population rises we need more land to populate, but that's not the way nature works. When a population gets too big, many of the animals die off. Not all, but many, & those left are strong, & they're the ones who survive to repopulate. That's how nature works in animals, & a human is just a thinking animal. We've populated the entire Earth, nature will strengthen the race.

KILLING OFF
THE PLANET

IT MIGHT NOT be that bad yet. Just because all the exotic large animals are facing extinction, & became endangered doesn't mean life on Earth is in danger completely. My dad was a farmer & we used to get 5 foot tall hay crops off one of his fields. While riding on the swather with him when he was cutting hay there, some of the weirdest bugs used to fly out of the hay as he was cutting it. They would land on your hand or your arm & you gotta shake them off. Things I have never seen again.

All big cats are endangered but there's a bunch of little animals there to take their place. The big cats, & the elephants are decendents of saber tooth tigers, & mammoths, but just because the Earth isn't suitable for them any more doesn't mean it's not suitable for something else. Because, the mammals took the place of the big reptiles, & something new will take the mammals place when hair becomes unnecissary to keep warm on a hotter planet.

I once saw a drawing on Canada AM of what reptile man would look like. It looked like a Teenage Mutant Ninja Turtle without a shell. That's what we would look like if we were decended from the dinosaurs, but we're not. Canada is very imaginative, & clever, & good at edjucating their children. Again, it might not be that bad yet, & It's not too late, according to the scientists. My dad gave me dinosaur books to learn to read on, not Bible stories. I know a thing or two about scientific observation. Science is the power of observation, & I've observed some weird insects in the hay fields that will survive the heat better than a dog, or a big cat.

Mainly the big land animals, & the large sea animals are dying out because there's not enough room for them anymore. There's too many of us, & we've developed the land. So, they die out, & there's many different small animals left in natures repituar to take their place, birds for example.

Birds are our only living dinosaurs. Who's to say the dinosaurs won't comeback. Birds can live in the city because they eat insects. They can live in the country cause they eat seeds. They can be free anywhere because they fly, & they're hard to catch for predators. They migrate, & can move with the changing temperatures, & some large ones live up to 80 years. The ultimate survivors they fly crazily about, & live free to no avail. Just as long as you don't steal their eggs. They're warm blooded, & have the feathers to protect them in the cold. Yet, can miraculously move any time they like if it gets too hot or dry, & can live in the same places as humans & even eat our garbage. Birds rule, & that's that.

LITTLE SHOP OF HORRORS

WHENEVER I FIND a roach in my apartment, I feed it to my Venus Fly Trap. It's a good way to keep the pest population down. I can't help but wonder if once they're being digested by the plant, they emit some sort of signal, or chemical that warns other roaches to stay away because, I've seen a lot less of them since I started doing this.

A long time ago when I was sharing an apartment with my little brother, he was fermenting in the kitchen, & we had a large amount of fruit flies in the kitchen. He had fly paper up but only caught a few of the knats. I decided to go get a venus fly trap, & see if it would catch some of the bugs. Over night they all died because after the venus fly trap caught one or two & the rest of the fruit flies were frightened onto the fly paper & we killed them all.

Could it be that the plant or the bugs send out a signal frightening all the other bugs in the area to beware of the venus fly trap? I got this idea for the venus fly trap out of an anarhcist cookbook. Anarchy isn't just clever bombs & ways to bug your enemies. It's call kinds of remedies to try. So you can see the different results. This one is by far my favorite.

Anarchy might serve a purpose in a world gone wrong too, or help get there. Different ways of protesting things we don't believe in, direct action, & remedies for survival can be very helpfull in living & staying alive. Knowlege is power, & the more you know about anarchy the better. Knowing different than what the general population believes, because as Bad Religion once said, "The popular conscientious doesn't make it right". That can mean anything to you. I think it means things like Russia being involved in rigging the '16 election. I don't believe Russia had anything to do with it simply because Putin said they didn't. Why would he lie, but the US politicians are so bent on a scandal they'll dream up anything, better believe it. They treat polotics like a tabloid,

& steer the US people into believing anything. The American people are led into believeing in all kinds of publicity stunts in the form of scandals just to premote candidates in a teeter totter fashion. One politician is denounced for sexual immorality, & that gives 10 more the opportunity to take hold inside the government. Using a backstabbing, lying fashion to manipulat their way to the top, & this is not, I believe what the founding fathers had in mind of a more perfect union.

Anarchy works in the small community, & the United States is an attempt at anarchy in a very large scale with too many people. In a tribal situation anarchy worked because everybody knew everybody, & crimes were dealt with on an idividual basis. These days, we worship the king in a democracy, & expect to go to heaven. Not how the founding fathers intended it. That's why I'm dragging the bodies back to the room & feeding them to my talking venus fly trap.

CROWS NEST

THERE'S ALWAYS A few crows flying around my neighborhood in pairs, & I see them in 2's or 4's all over town. I sometimes think that they are always the same birds, & they probably are. Crows are amazingly smart, & talkative. In Brittian they have two of them always guarding Buckingham Pallace. As a Canadian it seems like these crows here are just hanging around to make sure this lonely Canadian is doing ok.

I like to feed them bread, & I talk to them when I see them outside. They've been noticable since I got out of High School and I started spending a lot more time alone. Especially here in Mount Vernon. Not when I lived in Bellingham. In Bellingham there were always pigeons. There were never any pigeons in Mount Vernon until Sunrise services addded a few, & started putting seeds out for them every day. I know because the only place that has any pigeins is right outside Sunrise Services. Bellingham has pigeons, & Mount Vernon has crows. That's the way it was, & will always be.

Back on Lopez Island there were swallows. Swallows will build mud nests under you eves. I haven't seen a swallow since we moved to the mainland in 1989. I did see a hawk carry off a squirl last year. It was being chased by a sea gull. You can kill a sea gull with a tablet of alka-selzer, they explode because they can't burp. What a horrible way to go.

These finches here aren't tropically colored. Which means they're a different variety than the ones Charles Darwin observed in The Galopagos Islands. Thusforth confirming that in an evergreen forest finches will develop different colored feathers to blend in with the brown & greens in this climate. We won't know for sure if evolution is for real until an animal evolves before our eyes though. That's why it's good we have photographs these days. So, scientists of the future can compare their animals with those of today, & cataloge an evolutionary change. Wait till that discovery comes. When an animal evolves on record. It's the gradual change see, that's so hard to recognize. A sudden change would be easy to see. A sudden change would be like a mutation. A gradual change is an evolution. Either one would be pretty neat. Let's start by asking, "How could all the animals be perfectly adapted to environments that we know have changed historically through fossil record, without evolving?".

IF WE RUN OUT OF TIME, IT'S OUR FAULT

SOCIETY USED TO be based on the idea that everybody had, "The right to live". People had their place in society, & were taken care of there. As we moved to a Capitalist society, people no longer have the right to live, & it's based more on the idea, "We don't want you here, go somewhere else". This worked when we had places to go like The Wild West, or places to send the criminals Like Australia. Since we don't have new places to go anymore, we have homeless populations building on the street, & the rich don't understand what's going on anymore.

Tourists come to Seattle, & are surprised to see tents everywhere. Locals are getting used to it. These homeless would have been OK had they the right to live. Which they do not in a Capitalist society. The rich who are still taken care of can't understand why these people don't work. I can & it's because, all the good jobs are taken, & the meek jobs are held by migrants.

The migrants are holding the country together by doing the jobs none of the rich want to do, & the rich are taking all the easy jobs, & those in the working class who've given up on finding a job are now shoe'd away onto the street, & are hurting the tourism economy in Seattle.

Movies have been talking of going to space for a long time. Keep in mind, Congress has not approved funding for The Space Force. So, that was just an idea, & won't be a reality. We're gonna have to give the simple common man the right to live again, & a place to be taken care of.

WHAT REALLY KILLED THE DINOSAURS

I T MAY HAVE been a meteor, & it may not have been the dust & particles blocking out the sun that killed the dinosaurs. The dinosaurs may have gotten a disease from whatever amoebic life was on the meteor. Just like the smallpox blankets the white man gave the Native Americans that killed so many of them in the Indian wars.

The white man infected blankets with smallpox & gave the blankets to the Natives. The Natives thought it was OK until they got smallpox from the blankets. Their immune systems weren't strong enough to fight the disease, & many of them died.

We think there might be life on other planets at a cellular level. There may also be life on asteroids, & meteors. The scientists think they found the crater in Mexico City of whatever caused the dinosaurs extinction. There may have been life, & a disease on that meteor that the dinosaurs were not immune to. That's what may have killed them. That's what I believe.

IT'S HARD BEING EVIL WHEN THERE'S NO GOD

IN ENGLISH CLASS in the 4th grade, some of us were a little smarter than others at our school. So, they broke up the subjects into different classes rather than the students. I was in the 6th grade reading level class in the 4th grade. We learned about metaphores in our English class.

It's painfully obvious the bible was written to be interpereted metaphorically rather than litterally. "For god so loved the world he gave his only begotten son?" Metaphorically, if people need help, send somebody who matters to you, who knows what they're doing, to help, & make sure they're willing work themselves to death. That's an example of a metaphor. The bible is full of them.

There is no god in the sky. The author of the bible was just writing so that fools would be decieved. You can't fool everybody though. They don't fool me, & I won't waste my life in church. The author of the bible was smart though, she didn't use her name. Just like I don't, Goose Punk isn't my real name now is it?

www.ingramcontent.com/pod-product-compliance
Lightning Source LLC
Chambersburg PA
CBHW031430250726
48656CB00002B/914